P9-DCM-813

BEAR AWARE

Third Edition

Bill Schneider

FALCON®

GUILFORD, CONNECTICUT
HELENA, MONTANA

AN IMPRINT OF THE GLOBE PEQUOT PRESS

ΛFALCONGUIDE®

Illustrations by Kirk Botero
Text design by Lisa Reneson

ISSN 1549-0386
ISBN 0–7627–3108-7

Manufactured in the United States of America
Third Edition/First Printing

Contents

Books by Bill Schneider

Where the Grizzly Walks (1977, rev. ed. 2004)

Hiking Montana (1979, 3d ed. 2004)

The Dakota Image (1980)

The Yellowstone River (1985)

Best Hikes on the Continental Divide (1988)

The Flight of the Nez Perce (1988)

The Tree Giants (1988)

Hiking the Beartooths (1995)

Bear Aware (1996, 3d ed. 2004)

Hiking Carlsbad Caverns and Guadalupe Mountains National Parks (1996)

Best Easy Day Hikes Yellowstone (1997, 2d ed. 2003)

Exploring Canyonlands and Arches National Parks (1997)

Hiking Yellowstone National Park (1997, 2d ed. 2003)

Backpacking Tips (1998)

Best Easy Day Hikes Beartooths (1998)

Best Easy Day Hikes Grand Teton (1999)

Hiking Grand Teton National Park (1999)

Best Backpacking Vacations Northern Rockies (2002)

Hiking the Absaroka-Beartooth Wilderness (2003)

Best Easy Day Hikes Absaroka-Beartooth Wilderness (2003)

Learn more about Bill Schneider's books at
www. billschneider.net

Preface
Two Sides to Every Story

We are apprehensive that as more people
make use of the bears' shrinking domain,
an increase in bear attacks or maulings might
precipitate a reaction that could result in
wholesale destruction of the animals.

—Frank C. Craighead Jr.

Statistically, you're very safe from bears. Following the guidelines in this book will reduce the likelihood of your becoming a statistic even more. Bears definitely add an additional risk to your outdoor trip, but you take a much greater risk driving to the trailhead. And even if you do die on your hike, you're much more likely to drown, fall off a cliff, suffer heart failure or other sudden illness, or succumb to hypothermia.

Auto accidents, some very grisly, claim thousands of lives every year, but the news stories about them get buried deep within the daily newspaper. However, a bear mauling commands front-page headlines, and we read every word, right? This phenomenon won't change, but we must be careful to keep the danger posed by bears in perspective.

Domestic dogs kill more people than bears do. So do bees, Hereford bulls, mosquitoes, and lightning. Walking the streets of a big city is much more hazardous than walking in bear country. Central Park is more dangerous than Yellowstone Park.

Yes, bears have caused human injury and death. Hopefully, however, with the distribution of more information on how to safely hike and camp in bear country, fewer and fewer bears will make the front page and more and more people can safely enjoy the wilderness.

That's our side of the story. There's also the other side, the bears' side.

Carelessness can kill not only you and me, but also the bear. Most bear attacks result in dead bears.

In many cases, such as a surprise encounter in which a female causes human injury while protecting her cubs, rangers and wildlife managers take no action against the bear. However, in cases where the bear has lost its fear of humankind, bear managers have little choice but to designate the bear a dangerous offender and kill it. Or, arguably worse, they take the bear from the wild and banish it for life in a research lab, zoo, or drive-through wildlife park.

In certain circumstances a bear gradually becomes more conditioned to human food or garbage. Once a bear picks up this bad habit, it's a slow, but virtually guaranteed, death—a fed bear is a dead bear. The bear might stave off its fate for years, but sooner or later it crosses over the line, and authorities "remove it from the population." Obviously, bear encounters pose a threat to human safety. However, they also pose a threat to bear safety—and not just the safety of individual bears, but of the entire population.

This side of the story doesn't make many headlines; however, it's another reason we should take every possible precaution to avoid an encounter. Too many bear encounters could even lead to a movement to rid the forests of bears.

Therefore, there are two reasons for this book. This book might save you, and it might save a bear, too.

* * *

The original edition of *Bear Aware,* written in 1996, went through a minor revision in 2001. Since then, however, the science of bear–human encounters has changed significantly.

The use of bear pepper spray has earned the support of leading bear scientists. Prior to 2001, it was a widely accepted theory that pepper spray rarely worked. Now we know it does. Along with this approval came new recommendations for how to use bear pepper spray, which are included in this updated edition.

Previously, this book and others on the subject recommended different human reactions to black bears and grizzly bears. Now, bear experts say, "read the behavior, not the species." This new wave of thinking resulted in a nearly complete rewrite of the Close Encounters chapter.

I've also added updated information about research findings on attractants and deterrents. You may be surprised to learn what can attract bears, from colorful tents to plastic water bottles. Lastly, the list of resources in the appendix has been significantly expanded to help you find the safety gear and information you need. Enjoy it, and please be bear aware.

Acknowledgments

This book is much more than the work of one author. Through the years I have spent many hours discussing this subject with researchers, wildlife managers, park rangers, and leaders of environmental groups. The number of people who contributed to this book are too numerous to list.

I do, however, want to give special thanks to a few of the people who helped me research and review the book: Tom Smith of the Alaska Biological Science Center, Steve Herrero of the University of Calgary, Kerry Gunther of Yellowstone National Park, Gary Moses of Glacier National Park, Bill Stiver of Great Smoky Mountains National Park, Steve Cain of Grand Teton National Park, Christine Cowles of Yosemite National Park and Janet Breau from Parks Canada, Tom Puchlerz from the Northern Region of the USDA Forest Service, Chris Servheen of the U.S. Fish and Wildlife Service's Interagency Grizzly Bear Team, Chuck Bartlebaugh of the Center for Wildlife Information, long-time bear scientist Chuck Jonkel, and Patti Sowka from the Living with Wildlife Foundation.

The impetus for this book and many of the questions it answers came from the hundreds of people, too numerous to name, who attended my classes on hiking and camping in bear country at the Yellowstone Institute and other seminars on bear awareness.

I also want to thank the illustrator, Kirk Botero, and the staff of The Globe Pequot Press for doing such a superb job on the book.

Bear Sense

Your best weapon to minimize the risk of a bear attack is your brain. Use it as soon as you contemplate a trip to bear country, and continue to use it throughout your stay.

—Steve Herrero

One reason it's difficult to separate fact from fiction is that bears have a way of proving the experts wrong. As soon as somebody says, "Bears never do this," a bear comes along and does it. So don't generalize, and be wary of any absolute statement about bears.

Knowledge is the best defense. Outdoor people who know about bears have already taken the vital first step. They know what kind of equipment to bring, how to set up camp, when and where to be most careful, and which bear and human behaviors increase the chance of a bear attack. Since every bear encounter is different, the well informed can more easily improvise and deal with every situation. To help boost your knowledge, here are the answers to a few of the most commonly asked questions about bears.

Is there any way to be absolutely safe?

No. There is no way to guarantee total safety while traveling in bear country. However, you can greatly minimize the risk of being injured.

What's the difference between black bears and grizzly bears?

Black bears and grizzly bears differ significantly. From one important perspective, however, they are similar: Both species are dangerous. One common—and serious—mistake is thinking that only grizzlies are dangerous. Although the protocol for dealing with encounters differs between black bears and grizzlies, all bears are dangerous and should be treated as such.

A typical bear is as mythical as a typical person.

In fact, black bears cause more injuries than grizzly bears do, but grizzlies cause more serious injuries and fatalities. This is largely due to the fact that North America has more black bears in more places, but it's also partly due to people's nonchalant attitudes toward black bears. Never view a black bear as "Yogi" or "Smokey." Instead, view black bears as dangerous wild animals. North America has about fifty black bears for every grizzly bear, but each species is responsible for approximately one-half of the total fatalities traced to bears. One could interpret this disproportion to say grizzly bears are more dangerous than black bears, but, obviously, both species are dangerous.

Black bears and grizzlies commonly share the same habitat, and sometimes identification can be difficult, another reason to treat all bears as one dangerous species. Even though identification of certain bears can be difficult, the two species differ in many ways. See the graphics on pages 4–7.

Do bears stay in the same place or do they move around?

Both. Some bears stay close to a specific habitat while others range widely, as much as 50 miles per day. Habitat, reproductive status, and food supply dictate bear movement. Bears usually stay close to a good food source.

Never assume "there aren't any bears around here," and keep in mind that you can find bears anywhere in their range. As they say, bears are where they find you.

What do bears eat?

Almost anything. Bears are technically called carnivores, but they are primarily vegetarians and would best be called omnivores. They might also be called opportunists, since they almost always go for the easiest available meal, meat or vegetable.

Along the salmon streams of Alaska and Canada, bears commonly feast on the rich food supply provided by spawning salmon. But in most inland areas, bears feed primarily on foliage, roots, insects, nuts, and berries. Bears also hunt and kill large animals, but not as much as you might think. Some studies have found that the vast majority of a bear's diet is vegetative matter. So, you're much more likely to see a bear grazing like an elk than chasing an elk down for dinner.

How do bears know where you are?

Bears primarily use their sense of smell to detect danger or food. However, they also have excellent hearing. Bears have better vision than commonly believed, but they don't use their eyes nearly as much as their nose or ears.

Grizzly Bear

Ursus arctos

Color: Black to blond, frequently silver-tipped, giving a grizzled appearance.

Size: About 3–4 feet tall at shoulder, often over 6–8 feet tall when standing, 200 to 700 pounds in interior areas, and up to 1,200 pounds in coastal areas.

Distinguishing features: Prominent hump over shoulders, sloping back line, dished or concave face, large head, long curved claws that are usually light-colored and rarely less than 1.75 inches long.

Grizzly Bear Range

Grizzly Bear

Black Bear

Ursus americanus

Color: Black to blond, but usually with a muzzle that's a lighter color than the body, often with a white patch on throat or chest.

Size: About 2–4 feet tall at shoulder, about 4–5 feet tall when standing, 150 to 500 pounds.

Distinguishing features: Small size, straight facial profile, straight back line, small head, shorter claws that are usually dark-colored and rarely more than 1.5 inches long.

Black Bear Range

Black Bear

Note: Even bear experts have a hard time distinguishing between a small grizzly and a large black bear. Size and color cannot be used to identify bears. Treat all bears as dangerous wild animals.

A leaf fell in the woods.
The eagle saw it.
The deer heard it.
And the bear smelled it.

Why don't bears just stay away from people?

They try to, but they can't. There are virtually no places left just for bears. More and more people forge deeper and deeper into the remotest country, so bears can't stay away from us or our camps, temporary or permanent.

How can you tell if there are bears around?

Sometimes you can, but sometimes you can't. Bears leave signs, of course, such as scat, tracks, diggings, and bark ripped off trees. Try to familiarize yourself with these signs before going into bear country. If you haven't seen any bear sign, however, don't assume there aren't any bears around; bears are secretive and wide-ranging and can live near people without being seen.

How dangerous are bears?

All bears should be viewed as dangerous. Statistically, though, they aren't very dangerous—at least compared to other threats to human life. Actually, statistics can also be dangerous. Be careful not to rely on them too much, since the numbers can give you false confidence that might prompt you to skip some of the precautions recommended later in this book. Also, some statistics are only the best estimates of bear experts.

North America probably has 500,000 to 600,000 bears, mostly black bears. Yet, to date, bears have killed fewer than fifty people, an average of less than one person per year. For each recorded fatality caused by bears (all species), there are approximately 8 caused by spiders, 13 by snakes, 34 by domestic dogs, 90 by bees and wasps, and 190 by lightning.

Even national parks with large grizzly populations average fewer than one fatality per year—and millions of people visit these national parks annually.

Bear Mythology: Have You Heard This One?

But is the grizzly bear ferocious? All the first-hand
evidence I can find says he is not. Speaking from
years of experience with him my answer is emphati-
cally, No! During the greatest part of my life, I have
lived in a grizzly bear region. I have camped for
months alone and without a gun in their territory. I
have seen them when alone and when with hunters.
In Colorado, Utah, Arizona, Mexico, Wyoming,
Montana, Idaho, Washington, British Columbia and
Alaska, I have spent weeks trailing and watching
grizzlies, and their tracks in the snow showed that
they trailed me. They frequently came close, and
there were times when they might have attacked me
with every advantage. But they did not do so. As they
never made any attack on me, nor on anyone else
that I know of who was not bent on killing them, I
can only conclude that they are not ferocious.

—Enos Mills

People die. Bears die. But some of the old myths about
bears never seem to die. Some myths have persisted so
long that they seem like fact when, in reality, they're
either pure fiction or a severe stretching of the facts. Here
are a few examples.

Myth: **Bears are slow**

Reality check: Bears sometimes look slow, but that's as far from the truth as you can get. Bears can sprint 35 to 40 miles per hour for a short distance, faster than a racehorse and fast enough to run down an elk or deer—and about twice as fast as the fastest human being.

Myth: **Bears can't run downhill**

Reality check: Bears can run extremely fast uphill and downhill. Just because bears have shorter front legs than hind legs certainly doesn't mean they have trouble running in any terrain.

Myth: **Bears can't climb trees**

Reality check: Actually, mature grizzly bears can climb almost any tree (even trees with branch-free trunks), but they rarely do so, probably because it's difficult. If you can easily climb the tree, then the mature grizzly bear probably can, too. Mature grizzlies can reach 15 feet up a tree. Young grizzlies can climb trees, and all black bears can proficiently climb trees—and frequently do.

Myth: **Bears can't see**

Reality check: As near as scientists can determine, bears can see about as well as humans can. One theory suggests that bears commonly see better when young and suffer from failing vision in old age. Sound familiar?

Myth: **Bears are afraid of dogs**

Reality check: Some dogs chase bears, but these dogs are rarely "man's best friend" lying around the house most of the year waiting for those one or two weeks when they can come along to "protect" you on your outdoor vacation. More commonly, bears chase or kill dogs, an excellent reason not to take Fido on your wilderness trek. Your dog might run across a bear, and the bear could chase your "best friend" back to its master, and then, of course, you would have a big problem. Any dog in bear country must be carefully controlled and not allowed to run free.

Most national parks prohibit dogs in the backcountry, so be sure to check regulations before you consider taking your dog along.

Myth: **Black bears aren't dangerous**

Reality check: All bears are dangerous, but statistically, black bears may be more dangerous than grizzly bears. Black bears have injured more people than grizzlies have, and black bears inhabit more areas than grizzlies do, increasing your chances of encountering a bear.

Myth: **Bears aren't found around developed areas**

Reality check: You might find more bears around developed areas than you would in the remote backcountry. Bears can be very secretive. Just because you haven't seen bears around a developed area doesn't mean they aren't there.

Keep in mind that humans gravitate to the same high-quality habitat that bears do. We put our settlements along streams, in low country with rich soils and diverse vegetation. Bears and humans like the same places.

In addition, some people are still careless with garbage, allowing bears to feed on it. In some tourism developments, proprietors of hotels and restaurants actually feed bears on purpose to attract bear-watching tourists. These circumstances could make developed areas more dangerous than the deepest wilderness.

Myth: **Bears don't use trails**

Reality check: Bears frequently use trails because they offer the path of least resistance. You would not fight through thick underbrush when you could use a well-maintained trail, so why would a bear?

Myth: **Bears only come out at night**

Reality check: Bears are usually more active around dusk and dawn, but they can be active anytime during the day or night, especially on cool, wet days or during the early spring or late fall.

Myth: **Bears can't swim**

Reality check: Bears love water and are excellent swimmers.

Myth: **Horses attract bears**

Reality check: Nobody knows for sure if horses attract or deter bears (or neither), but horses normally make more noise on the trail than hikers do. Horses also sense bears before we do, so it's more likely that horses are a deterrent.

There isn't a single recorded incident of a backcountry traveler being mauled by a bear while riding a horse. However, a few people have been hurt after being thrown from a horse spooked by a bear.

Myth: **Smoke from campfires attracts bears**

Reality check: There is no scientific evidence to support this, nor have there been any encounters linked to campfire smoke. It's just as likely that campfire smoke serves as a deterrent by alerting bears for miles around of your presence. However, cooking over a campfire (as opposed to a backpacking stove) could more widely disperse food odors and, perhaps, attract bears. Also, partially burned food in fire pits could attract bears. Never burn leftovers unless you're positive the campfire will stay hot enough long enough to completely burn all food and destroy all odors.

Myth: **Bears are always afraid of people**

Reality check: Although most bears are indeed afraid of people—or at least try hard to avoid us—there are exceptions. Bear populations in some national parks may, for example, be gradually losing, generation by generation, their fear of humans. Each year a few bears display behavior that clearly shows they have lost their fear and may be more dangerous. Never assume all bears will flee instantly.

Hiking in Bear Country

Are grizzly bears killers? I would have to say no. If the grizzly bear were half as bad as commonly portrayed, early explorers and frontiersmen would not have gotten far across the prairies, and the opening of the West would likely have been delayed until the advent of the repeating rifle.

—Andy Russell

The first step of any hike in bear country is an attitude adjustment. Nothing guarantees total safety. Hiking in bear country adds a small risk to your trip. However, that risk can be greatly minimized by adhering to this age-old piece of advice—be prepared. And being prepared doesn't only mean having the right equipment. It also means having the right knowledge. Knowledge is the best defense.

Don't let fear ruin your trip

You can—and should—thoroughly enjoy your trip to bear country. Don't let the fear of bears ruin your vacation. This fear can accompany you every step of the way. It can constantly lurk in the back of your mind, preventing you from enjoying the wildest and most beautiful places left on Earth. And even worse, some bear experts think bears might actually be able to sense your fear.

Being prepared and knowledgeable gives you confidence. It allows you to fight back the fear that can haunt you throughout your stay in bear country. You won't—nor should you—forget about bears and the basic rules of safety, but proper preparation allows you to keep the fear of bears at bay and let enjoyment rule the day.

Do you really want to be totally safe?

If we really wanted to be totally safe, we probably would never go hiking in the wilderness—bears or no bears. We certainly wouldn't—at much greater risk—drive hundreds of miles to get to the trailhead. Perhaps a tinge of danger adds a desired element to our wilderness trip.

The five basic rules of hiking safely in bear country

Nobody likes surprises, and bears dislike them, too. The majority of bear maulings occur when a hiker surprises a bear. Therefore, it's vital to do everything possible to avoid these surprise meetings, starting with "The Basic Five."

---

1. *Be alert.*
2. *Go in a large group and stay together.*
3. *Stay on the trail.*
4. *Hike in the middle of the day.*
5. *Make noise.*

If you follow these five rules, the chance of encountering a bear on the trail sinks to the slimmest possible margin.

Defensive driving works. So does defensive hiking.

No substitute for alertness

As you hike, watch ahead and to the sides. Don't fall into the all-too-common and particularly nasty habit of fixating on the trail a few feet ahead. It's especially easy to do this when dragging a heavy pack up a long hill or when carefully watching your step on a rocky or eroded trail.

Using your knowledge of bear habitat and habits, be especially alert in areas most likely to be frequented by bears, such as avalanche chutes, berry patches, along streams, through stands of whitebark pine, in salmon spawning areas, and so on.

Watch carefully for bear signs and be especially watchful (and noisy) if you see any. If you see a track or scat but it doesn't look fresh, pretend it's fresh. The area is obviously frequented by bears.

Watch the wind

The wind can be friend or foe. The direction and strength of the wind can make a significant difference in your chances of an encounter with a bear.

When the wind blows on your back, you're much safer, since your smell travels ahead of you, alerting any bear on or near the trail ahead. Conversely, when the wind blows on your face, your chances of a surprise meeting with a bear increase, because a bear can't smell you coming, so make more noise and be more alert.

A strong wind can also be noisy and limit a bear's ability to hear you coming. If a bear can't smell or hear you coming, the chances of an encounter greatly increase, so watch the wind.

Safety in numbers

There have been very few instances where a large group has had a serious encounter with a bear. On the other hand, a large percentage of hikers mauled by bears were hiking alone or with one other person. Large groups naturally make more noise and put out more smell and probably appear more threatening to bears. In addition, if you're hiking alone and get injured, there's nobody to go for help. For these reasons, some national parks recommend parties of four or more hikers when going into bear country.

If a large party splits up, it becomes two or more small parties, and the advantage is lost. So stay together. If you're on a family hike, keep the kids from running ahead. If you're in a large group, keep the stronger members from going ahead or weaker members from lagging behind. The best way to prevent this natural separation is to ask one of the slowest members of the group to lead. This keeps everybody together.

People are supposed to be on trails

Although bears use trails, they don't often use them during midday when hikers commonly use them. Through generations of associating trails with people, bears probably expect to find hikers on trails, especially during midday. On infrequently used trails, however, it may be more likely to find a bear using the trail or bedded down on or near the trail. Contrarily, bears probably don't expect to find hikers off trails. Bears rarely settle down in a day bed right along a well-used trail. However, if you wander around in thickets off the trail, you might stumble into an occupied day bed or cross paths with a traveling bear.

Sleeping late has its rewards

Bears—and most other wildlife—usually aren't active during the middle of the day, especially on a hot summer day. Wild animals are most active around dawn and dusk. Therefore, hiking early or late increases your chances of seeing wildlife, including bears. Likewise, hiking in the middle of a hot day reduces the chance of an encounter.

Sometimes, it's okay to be loud and obnoxious

Perhaps the best way to avoid an encounter is to make sure the bear knows you're there, so make lots of noise. However, the best type of noise is a source of debate.

One theory supports metallic noise, such as bear bells, pebbles in a can, aluminum fly rod case, or metal-tipped walking stick clanged on trailside rocks, as the best. Metallic noise doesn't occur in nature, so it must come from humans, so the theory goes, and is less likely to be muffled by natural conditions than human voices. Other bear experts, however, think that human voices rather than metallic noise are more likely to alert bears of your presence. One recent research project in Alaska found that bears more or less ignored both metallic noise (bear bells) and human voices unless these sounds were unusually loud, but were alerted immediately by the sound of snapping sticks and bear-like growls. Loud clapping tends to sound like twigs breaking and has been effective in alerting bears.

All bear experts recommend making noise, but you have to make the decision on what *type* of noise. One way to make the decision easier is to check at the local ranger station, which often gives out specific recommendations.

Sometimes, it's not okay to be loud and obnoxious

While planning your noise making, be sure to discuss respect for other hikers—or as some experts call it, "appropriate noise." Hikers hike to get away from "noise pollution," so keep in mind that some conditions warrant silence to better enjoy wild nature. For example, if you're closely following another group of hikers up the trail, you can forego noise making. The same goes in places where there's no chance of seeing a bear, such as open stretches of trail through tundra or alpine meadows or trails gouged out of cliff faces where you can see a long distance up the trail. You can safely remain quiet and enjoy the wilderness in these situations and then yell or clap loudly when you approach a thicket or brushy ravine. Also, please preserve everybody's wilderness experience by not making loud noises in camp.

You don't need a better view

If you see a bear, don't try to get closer for a better look. The bear might interpret this as an act of aggression and charge.

Use a longer lens instead

A high percentage of people mauled by bears are photographers. That's because they're purposely being quiet hoping to see wildlife. In some cases they try to get closer to a bear for a better photo. Such behavior is counter to all rules for traveling safely in bear country—and threatens the bear, too, which are often killed after being involved in a serious encounter.

Running up the risk

Many avid runners like to get off paved roads and running tracks and onto backcountry trails. But running on trails in bear country can be seriously hazardous to your health.

Most runners avoid running during the heat of the day. Instead, they run early or late in the day when bears are most active. Runners rarely make enough noise when running, and they might even sound like a wild animal (i.e., prey for bears) running on a trail. Fervent trail runners know that you tend to get closer to wildlife running than you do walking. Some people think that's because you cover distance faster than expected by wildlife. Other people think it's because you tend to be quieter when running. Whatever the reason, running on trails obviously increases your chance of surprising a bear.

The best advice is to avoid running in bear country, but if you're a hopelessly addicted runner and can't resist trying a scenic trail in bear country, at least strap a bell on your fanny pack.

Leave the night to the bears

Like running on trails, hiking at night can be very risky. Bears are more active after dark, and you can't see them until it's too late. If you get caught out at night, be sure to make lots of noise.

You can be dead meat, too

If you see or smell an animal carcass when hiking, immediately vacate the area. Don't let your curiosity keep you near the carcass a second longer than you need to recognize this as an extremely dangerous situation.

Bears commonly hang around a carcass, guarding it and feeding on it for days until it's consumed. Your presence easily could be interpreted as a threat to the bear's food supply, and a vicious attack could be imminent.

If you see a carcass ahead of you on the trail, don't go any closer. Instead, abandon your hike and return to the trailhead. If the carcass is between you and the trailhead, take a very long detour around it, upwind from the carcass, making lots of noise along the way. Be sure to report the carcass to the local ranger or game warden. This tip might prompt a temporary trail closure or special warnings but might also prevent injury to other hikers and the death of a bear. Rangers will, in some cases, go in and drag the carcass away from the trail, but usually they'll temporarily close the area.

Cute, cuddly, and lethal

The same advice for approaching carcasses also goes for bear cubs. If you see one, don't go one inch closer. The cub might seem abandoned, but most likely it's not. Mother bear is probably close by, and female bears fiercely defend their young.

Side trips

Many backpackers like to take a side trip during a long day to see a special place or enjoy a few hours without the heavy pack. If you do this, be sure to hang your pack out of reach of bears in much the same manner you would hang your food at night. If you don't take the time to do this, you might end up with, at the least, a destroyed backpack and, at the worst, an encounter with a bear defending the food reward it found in your pack. You could also be doing a great disservice to future backpackers by conditioning a bear to look for food in stashed backpacks.

As a fringe benefit, you won't have holes chewed in your pack by rodents.

Regulations are for your (and the bears') safety

Nobody likes rules and regulations. However, national parks and forests have a few that you must follow. These rules aren't meant to take the freedom out of your trip. They're meant to help bring you back safely—and to keep bears wild—and alive.

When you get a backcountry camping permit in a national park, you get a list of these rules. In some cases, they're printed right on your permit. In national forests you usually don't need a permit, but you can check with the local ranger for any special regulations. In both national parks and national forests, carefully read the notices on the information boards at trailheads.

But I didn't see any bears!

Now you know how to be safe. Walk up the trail constantly clanging two metal pans together. It works every time. You won't see a bear, but you'll hate your "wilderness experience." You left the city to get away from loud noise.

Yes, you can be very, very safe, but how safe do you want to be and still be able to enjoy your trip? It's a balancing act. First, be knowledgeable and then decide how far you want to go. Everybody has to make his or her own personal choice.

Here's another conflict. If you do everything recommended in this book, you most likely won't see any bears—or any deer or moose or eagles or any other wildlife. Again, you make the choice. If you want to be as safe as possible, follow these rules religiously. If you want to see wildlife, including bears, only make noise when necessary and don't use bear bells and, in general, do all of the recommendations in this chapter in reverse. If you make this choice, you are, of course, increasing your chances of an encounter instead of decreasing them.

The Bear Essentials
Hiking in Bear Country

Knowledge is the best defense.

There is no substitute for alertness.

Hike with a large group and stay together.

Don't hike alone in bear country.

Stay on the trail.

Hike in the middle of the day.

Make lots of noise.

Never approach a bear.

Cubs are deadly.

Stay away from carcasses.

Defensive hiking works; try it.

Know and adhere to regulations.

Camping in Bear Country

Already our studies were revealing that the grizzly did not fear man but preferred to avoid him when possible and, as other bear–man confrontations showed, to combat him if necessary.
—Frank C. Craighead Jr.

Staying overnight in bear country is not dangerous, but it adds a slight additional risk to your trip. The main differences between day trips into bear country and camping in bear country are more food, cooking, and garbage. Plus, you're in bear country at a time when bears are usually most active. Once again, however, following a few basic rules greatly minimizes this risk.

Get a permit

Most national parks require backpackers to have a backcountry camping permit. One reason for this system is safety. If a bear has been raiding camps in one area in the park, rangers probably won't allow any overnight camping there.

Backcountry campsite reservation systems also provide an opportunity to discuss the bear situation with a knowledgeable ranger. After you select a campsite, ask the ranger about bear activity in the area. In some cases you can get brochures or watch a short video on camping in bear country.

Most national forests don't have designated campsites, but it's still wise to stop in at the local ranger station and ask about bear activity before heading for the trailhead.

Selecting a campsite

Bears and people often like the same places, which makes selecting a good campsite an important decision.

Sometimes, you have little to say about where you camp. If you're backpacking in a national park, regulations probably require that you stay in a precisely located campsite reserved in advance. The National Park Service considers the bear situation when designating campsites, and discussing the bear situation with the ranger might prompt you to choose one site over another.

In most national forests and some national parks such as Yosemite and Denali, you can camp anywhere. Regulations might require you to camp certain distances from water or trails, but you aren't confined to a specific campsite.

When you get there

When you get to your campsite, immediately think about bears. Look around for bear signs. If you see fresh sign, move on to another site with no signs of bear activity. If you see a bear in or near the campsite, don't camp there—even if you're in a national park and you have reserved this campsite. If you have time before nightfall, return to the trailhead and report the incident to a ranger. If it's getting late, you have little choice but to camp at an undesignated site and report it to the ranger after you finish the hike. Safety always prevails over regulations. Don't get yourself in a situation where you have to hike or set up camp in the dark.

Being careful not to camp in a campsite frequented by bears is perhaps the most important precaution you can take. Unfortunately, people who cause a bear to become conditioned to human food or garbage are rarely the people who get injured by that bear. The person who is injured usually comes along later and unknowingly camps in the same site where a bear has become accustomed to getting human food.

Look for signs of previous campers. If you see food scraps, litter, and other signs that the previous campers might not have used proper bear-country camping techniques, you might want to choose another campsite.

Plan your hike so you aren't setting up camp a half-hour before nightfall, which doesn't leave time to move to another campsite if necessary. If you set up camp in the dark, you have little chance to check around for bear signs or signs of previous campers.

Key features of a good campsite

One key feature of a good campsite in bear country is a place to store food. Most designated sites in national parks and in some national forests have a food storage device or "bear pole." However, in most national forests and in some national parks, you're on your own, so scout the campsite for trees that can serve as a food storage device. You need a tree at least 100 yards from your tent with a large branch, or two trees close enough to suspend your food between them on a rope. You can also use a tree that has partially fallen and is still leaning securely on other trees. In any case, however, the trees must be tall enough to get the food at least 10 feet off the ground and 4 feet from the tree trunk.

Choose a campsite away from popular fishing areas such as along salmon spawning streams or lake inlets. If previous campers fished close to camp, they may have left dead fish or fish entrails around camp, and the smell of fish definitely attracts bears. If you have fish for dinner, clean them at least 200 yards from camp and dispose of the entrails by throwing them into deep water.

Avoid camping along trails, streams, or lakeshores, which often serve as travel corridors for bears. Since bears like to travel and remain concealed in trees, camp in an open area. If possible, set your tent near an "escape" tree that you can climb in case a bear comes into camp, and make a mental note of its location so you can find it in the dark of night. Pick a tree that's not too easy to climb; you don't want it to be easy for the bear.

Try to avoid camping along a trail in or near thick brush or timber. Because dense vegetation makes travel more difficult for all animals, bears will likely use the trail as the path of least resistance and pass dangerously close to you during the night.

Setting up camp

Once you've found a good campsite, take the next crucial step of correctly setting up camp, which isn't as simple as it sounds. Some camping traditions can increase the chance of a bear entering your camping area.

You probably have seen photos of picturesque camping scenes with a family just outside the tent entrance sitting around the fire cooking dinner. Forget this. The sleeping area and the cooking area must be separated by at least 100 yards.

Zero-impact camping equals safe bear-country camping.

Try to set up the tent at least 100 yards upwind from the cooking area. Also, if possible, pitch the tent uphill from the cooking area. Since night breezes in the mountains usually blow downhill, the wind will carry food smells away from the sleeping area instead of over it.

Spreading out the camp might create some extra walking and inconvenience, but in the unusual circumstance that a bear does come into camp, it's likely to go straight for the smell of food—where you've been cooking and eating. So, obviously, you don't want to be sleeping there. Concentrate all food smells in the cooking area and keep them away from your sleeping area.

Park rangers encourage backpackers to hang or store food as close to the cooking area as possible, and in many designated campsites, rangers have strategically placed a "bear pole" or bear-resistant container for food storage near designated cooking areas. This practice helps concentrate all food smells in one area.

Get in the habit of separating cooking area items from sleeping area items in your backpack. Then, while setting up camp, you can conveniently separate articles into two piles.

For large parties, set up tents in the most secure areas and space them out linearly (not in a circular pattern). Put the most experienced people at each end of the line of tents.

Free sleeping invites disaster

National park visitors have been known to have a particularly nasty habit called "free sleeping." In an attempt to save money or when all the campgrounds are full, some visitors simply pull off the road in an undesignated camping area and pitch a tent or, even worse, just throw a sleeping bag out on the ground. Besides violating park regulations, this can be very dangerous. The "free sleeper" might be saving a few dollars, but he or she might also be unknowingly camping in an area heavily used by bears.

Not under the stars

Some people prefer to sleep out under the stars instead of using a tent. This might be okay in areas not frequented by bears, but it isn't a good idea in bear country. The thin fabric of a tent certainly isn't any real physical protection from a bear, but it does present a psychological barrier to a bear that wants to come even closer.

Storing food and garbage

If the campsite doesn't have an established food storage device (bear pole or metal box), be sure to set one up or at least locate one before it gets dark. It isn't only difficult to store food after darkness falls, but it's easier to forget some juicy morsel on the ground. Also, be sure to store food in airtight, waterproof bags to prevent food odors from circulating throughout the forest. For double pro-

A model campsite for camping in bear country.

tection, put food and garbage in zip-locked bags and then seal tightly in a larger plastic bag.

The illustrations on pages 35–36 depict three popular methods for hanging food. In any case, try to get food and garbage at least 10 feet off the ground.

Always try to keep food odors off your pack, but if you fail, put the food bag inside and hang the pack.

Store food and other scented items such as toothpaste, sunscreen, and water bottles (especially if they've ever been used for juice, lemonade, or fitness drinks) at least 100 yards from the tent. A few national parks such as Grand Teton recommend the "counter-balance" method of hanging food. Check on this when getting your back-country permit.

Special equipment

Zip-locked bags are perfect for keeping food smell to a minimum and helps keep food from spilling on your pack, clothing, or other gear. Be sure to also pack a special bag for hanging and storing food. The bag must be sturdy and waterproof. You can get drybags at most outdoor retailers, but you can get by with a trash compactor bag. Regular garbage bags are too flimsy and can break and leave your food spread on the ground.

There are several varieties of bear-resistant containers on the market, but they add unwanted weight to a pack. You can check out some of the new, lighter models, but in most cases, an airtight plastic bag will suffice. A few national parks, especially in Alaska, require bear-resistant food storage containers.

You also need 100 feet of nylon cord. You don't need a heavy climbing rope to store food. Go light instead. Parachute cord will usually suffice unless you plan to hang large quantities of food and gear, which could be the case on a long backpacking excursion with a large group.

You can also buy a small pulley system to make hoisting a heavy load easier. Again, you can usually get by without this extra weight in your pack unless you have a massive load to hang.

Getting the food up there

People get hurt hanging their food at night, so be careful.

The classic method is tying a rock or piece of wood to the end of your rope and tossing it over the branch and then attaching the rope to the bag or backpack and hoisting it up 10 feet or more. If the load gets too heavy, wrap it around a small tree or branch for leverage. To make this easier, take a small ditty bag and permanently attach at least 50 feet of nylon cord to it. Then, when you're at camp, instead of trying to tie a rock on the end of your rope, put rocks in the small bag, close it, and toss it over the branch or bear pole.

Use gloves so you don't get rope burn. And, of course, don't let the rock or wood come down on your head (it happens!). Also, don't let anybody stand under the bag until you're sure it's securely in place.

(As a footnote, be careful not to leave your rope behind the next morning. Once you've untied your food, slowly pull your rope over the branch. Don't jerk it. If the rope gets stuck and you can't climb the tree, you have to leave it behind.)

What to hang

Hang everything that has any food smell. This includes cooking gear, eating utensils, water bottles, bags used to keep food in your pack, garbage, and even clothes with food smells on them. If you spilled something on your clothes, change into other clothes for sleeping and hang clothes with food smells with the food and garbage. If you take them into the tent, you aren't separating your sleeping area from food smells. Also, hang scented non-food items like toothpaste, bug dope, and sunscreen.

Hanging food at night isn't the only storage issue. During the day make sure you place food correctly in your pack. Use airtight packages as much as possible. Store food in the containers it came in or, once opened, in zip-locked bags. This keeps food smells out of your pack and off your other camping gear and clothes.

What to keep in your tent

You can't be too careful in keeping food smells out of the tent. If a bear has become accustomed to coming into

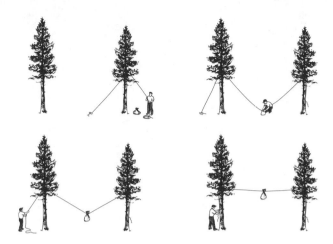

Steps for hanging food and garbage between two trees.

Steps for hanging food and garbage over tree branch.

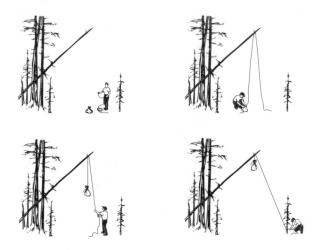

Steps for hanging food and garbage over leaning tree.

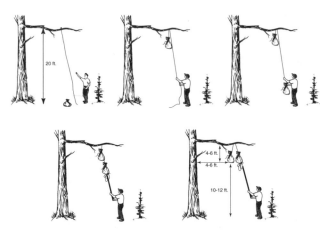

Steps for hanging food with the counter-balance method.

that campsite looking for food, it's vital for your protection to keep all food smells out of the tent. This often includes your pack, which is hard to keep odor-free. Usually only take valuables (such as cameras and binoculars), clothing, and sleeping gear into the tent—and, of course, bear spray. (See Chapter 5 for more information on bear spray.) Also, keep a flashlight in the tent. If an animal comes into camp and wakes you up, you need the flashlight to identify it.

Camping above timberline or treeline

Camping above timberline or north of the treeline make food storage difficult, so avoid this when possible. If you must camp in alpine or tundra areas, use a bear-resistant food container and store it at least 200 yards downwind and downhill from your sleeping area.

If you don't have a bear-resistant food container, your remaining options are far from ideal. Keep all food and garbage in zip-locked bags and then double bag it in large plastic bags. If you can find a cliff nearby, hang the double-bagged food over the cliff. If you can't find a cliff, put the bag on top of a large boulder to at least get it off the ground. One other option is to use a guaranteed waterproof bag and submerge food overnight.

The campfire

Regulations prohibit campfires in many areas, but if you're in a place where fires are allowed, treat yourself. Besides adding to the nightly entertainment, the fire might make your camp safer from bears.

The campfire provides the best possible way to get rid of food smells—as long as food scraps and garbage are totally burned away to ashes. Build a small but hot fire and burn everything that smells of food—garbage, leftovers, fish entrails, everything. Even if you brought food in cans or other incombustible containers, put them in the fire, too. You can even dump extra water from cooking or dishwater on the edge of the fire to erase the smell.

In the crowded wilderness of today, campfires are frequently disallowed and, if not, are rarely in line with the principles of zero-impact ethics. However, if you decide bear safety outweighs the zero-impact principles, be very sure you have the fire hot enough to completely burn everything. If you leave partially burned food scraps in the fire, you're setting up a dangerous situation for the next camper who uses this site.

Before leaving camp the next morning, dig out the fire pit and pack out anything that hasn't totally burned, even if you believe it no longer carries food smells. For example, many foods like dried soup or hot chocolate come in foil packages that might seem like they burn, but they really don't. Pack out the scorched foil and cans (now with very minor food smells). Also, pack out foil and cans left by other campers.

Burning leftovers in campfires is not allowed in some national forests and national parks, so be sure to check local regulations before heading for the trailhead. In most cases, you'll find the best advice listed at the trailhead information boards, which is "Pack it in, Pack it out."

Types of food

Don't get paranoid about the types of food you bring. All food has some smell, and you can make your trip much less enjoyable by fretting too much over food.

Perhaps the safest option is freeze-dried food. It carries very little smell, and freeze-dried food comes in convenient envelopes that allow you to cook it by merely adding boiling water, so you don't have cooking pans to wash or store. However, freeze-dried food is expensive, and many campers don't use it—and still safely enjoy bear country.

Dry, pre-packed meals (often pasta- or rice-based) offer an affordable compromise to freeze-dried foods. Also, take your favorite high-energy snack and don't worry about it. Avoid fresh fruit and canned meats and fish.

What food you bring is much less critical than how you handle it, cook it, and store it. A can of tuna fish might put out a smell, but if you eat all of it in one meal, don't spill it on the ground or your clothes, and burn the can later, it can be quite safe.

How to cook

The overriding philosophy of cooking in bear country is to create as little odor as possible. Keep it simple. Use as few pans and dishes as possible.

Unless it's a weather emergency, don't cook in the tent. This creates food odors in the tent (the last thing you want when in bear country), and you face the threats of carbon monoxide poisoning and setting your tent on fire. If you like to winter camp, you might cook in the tent, but you need a four-season tent designed for this with adequate vents. In most cases, three-season tents aren't designed for cooking, so avoid cooking in them except in real emergencies.

If you can have a campfire and decide to cook fish, try cooking in aluminum foil envelopes instead of frying or roasting the fish over an open flame. Then, after removing the cooked fish, quickly burn the fish scraps off the foil. Using foil also means you don't have to wash the pan you used to cook the fish.

Also, manage fuel for your backpacking stove carefully. Fuel can be a strong bear attractant. Use a funnel and no-spill container when refilling stoves (and lanterns).

Leftovers

Try hard not to cook too much food, so you don't have to deal with leftovers. If you end up with extra food, you only have two choices: carry it out or burn it. Don't bury it or throw it in a lake or leave it anywhere in bear country. A bear most likely will find and dig up any food or garbage buried in the backcountry.

Taking out the garbage

In bear country you have only two choices for dealing with garbage—burn it or carry it out. Since campfires are prohibited in many areas, prepare for garbage problems before leaving home. Bring along zip-locked bags to store garbage and carry in as little garbage as possible by discarding excess packaging.

Washing dishes

This is a sticky problem with only one easy solution. If you don't dirty dishes, you don't have to wash them. So try to minimize food smell by using as few dishes and pans as possible—or better yet, none at all. If you use the principles of zero-impact camping, you're probably doing as much as you can to reduce food smell from dishes.

If you brought paper towels, use one to carefully remove food scraps from pans and dishes before washing them. Then, when you wash dishes, you'll have much less food smell. Burn the dirty towels or store them in zip-locked bags with other garbage. Put pans and dishes in zip-locked bags before putting them back in your pack.

If you end up with lots of food scraps in the dishwater, drain out the scraps and store them in zip-locked bags with other garbage, or burn them. You can bring a lightweight screen to filter out food scraps from dishwater, but be sure to store the screen with the food and garbage. If you don't have a screen, use your bandana. If you have a campfire, pour the dishwater around the edge of the fire. If you don't have a fire, take the dishwater at least 100 yards downwind and downhill from camp and pour it on the ground. Don't put dishwater or food scraps in a lake or stream.

Finally, don't put it off. Do dishes immediately after eating to minimize food smells.

Although possibly counter to accepted rules of cleanliness for many people, you can skip washing dishes altogether on the last night of your trip. Instead, simply use the paper towels to clean the dirty dishes as much as possible. You can wash them at home. Pack dirty dishes in airtight bags before putting them in your pack.

Dog and horse food

It's usually unwise to take dogs into bear country, and it's prohibited in many national parks. If you do it anyway, treat the dog food like human food. Store it in airtight bags, and hang it at night.

Although horses don't increase your risk of encountering a bear, the large amount of food necessary for horses does pose an additional risk. Again, treat horse food as carefully as you do human food. Horse pellets are like little candy bars to bears.

No safe sex

Although there is no real evidence to support this theory, some bear experts believe that human sexual activity attracts bears.

Vehicle camping

Don't have the attitude that vehicle campgrounds offer added security from bears. In some cases, the reverse might be true.

If you're sleeping in a tent, there isn't much difference between backcountry camping and camping in a vehicle campground. Be equally careful with food and garbage.

One advantage you have in a vehicle campground is easier food storage. Keep food and garbage in airtight containers and then store them in your vehicle at night or when not in use. Keep food smells out of the tent.

One disadvantage of vehicle campgrounds is the small size of the campsite. You can't effectively separate your sleeping area from your cooking area.

Look around for bear signs, and if you see any, go to another campsite. If you see a culvert trap in the area, it usually means rangers are trying to remove problem bears, a good tip-off to go elsewhere.

Attractants and repellents

Nobody really knows what attracts or repels bears, but everybody agrees on one thing. The smell of human food and garbage definitely attracts bears. If you don't want to attract bears, be extremely careful with food and garbage.

Bear experts also agree on two more things: bears have a supersensitive sense of smell, and they're curious. Given these two facts, it seems best to avoid anything that might prompt a bear to investigate. Try to blend into the natural environment instead of stand out from it. This means avoiding things like neon tents, backpacks, and clothing; camping in highly visible sites such as ridgelines or above timberline; making animal-like sounds; or, using any kind of strong scent. All of these things might excite a bear's curiosity. Some recent research has indicated, for example, that bears might be attracted to bright colors such as the yellow used in some backpacking tents and coats but ignore or barely notice dull, earth-tone colors, especially camouflage. At the same time, let's be realistic. There's no need, for example, to throw away your yellow tent, but instead, be careful not to display it loudly on a ridgeline where a bear can see it from a mile away. Don't present bears with a "visual cue" that they simply can't ignore and therefore must approach to investigate.

Likewise, researchers discovered that bears show interest in many strong scents, such as Citronella (an ingredient in some insect repellents), fruity shampoos and lip balms, fuel for backpacking stoves, and human urine and feces. There needs to be more research, but in the meantime, it seems prudent to try to minimize the scents associated with being human. (And, of course, don't relieve yourself too close to camp.)

If scientists could come up with the right scent, sound, or color to keep bears out of our camps, it would be a collective sigh of relief, but until that happens, don't take chances. Avoid bright colors, unusual or loud sounds, and strong smells. Obviously, hikers and campers aren't using anything now that actively attracts bears; if they were, there would have been many more encounters.

Do somebody you don't know a big favor

Report all bear sightings to the ranger after your trip. This might not help you, but it could save another camper's life—and it could save the life of a bear, too. If rangers get enough reports to spot a pattern, they will manage the area accordingly and not unknowingly allow camping in a potentially hazardous situation.

The Bear Essentials
Camping in Bear Country

Select a safe campsite.

Camp below timberline.

Separate cooking and sleeping areas.

Sleep in a tent.

Keep food odors out of the tent.

Cook the right amount of food and eat it all.

Store food and garbage out of the reach of bears.

Leave the campsite cleaner than you found it.

For Your Protection

Research clearly demonstrates that the normal response of grizzly bears is to avoid people and not to act aggressively or to attack, even if a person suddenly appears nearby.

—Steve Herrero

Protecting yourself from a bear is the second priority. The first priority is preventing a situation where you have to protect yourself.

Guns

Traditionally, travelers in bear country carried firearms, and in the hands of a skilled person, guns can offer the desired level of protection. Regrettably, the aftermath of this success is a dead bear.

In unskilled hands, however, guns can make the situation worse. You need a heavy caliber, and a misplaced shot can wound and infuriate a bear. Gun-handling experience is critical. If you take a gun, go to a gun expert and get good advice on what type of firearm to take. Then, get lots of practice.

Keep in mind that guns aren't an option in national parks. Most national parks prohibit carrying firearms on backcountry trails.

Loud noise

Guns can be used as noisemakers to scare off bears. The same goes for loudly banging pans together, firecrackers, air horns, and other loud noise. Loud noise is more likely to work with black bears than with grizzlies.

Bear spray

In recent years bear spray, which stings the eyes and hampers breathing, has earned more and more respect from experts. In one study of sixty-six encounters, many people escaped uninjured by turning away a charging bear with bear spray. Now, most park rangers carry it when in bear country. In no recorded case has bear spray made a bear more aggressive or harmed the bear. In fact, getting sprayed might make a bear more wary of humans.

Even though bear spray can help erase that deepseated fear that can ruin a trip to bear country, it has a downside. Bear spray, like firearms, can create a false sense of security. Having bear spray mounted on your belt or pack strap doesn't mean you can skip the precautions outlined in Chapters 3 and 4. Poor handling of food and garbage can get you (or other campers who follow you) into much more trouble than bear spray can solve. Canned pepper definitely does not make you bear-proof. Instead of being a cure-all, bear spray is merely your next-to-last line of defense. If it doesn't turn away the bear, your only remaining options are playing dead or physical resistance.

Here, point-by-point, are tips for using bear spray:

- Be sure you buy something called "Bear Spray" or "Bear Pepper Spray." Some products labeled "Pepper Spray" are not meant for use on bears.

✔ Before you leave the trailhead, read the directions on the bear spray container or packaging. If you're uncertain about how to operate the spray, buy an extra canister, test-fire it, and discard it. Then, hit the trail with a new full canister. (You can also get inexpensive test canisters from some companies to familiarize yourself with operating the spray.)

✔ If you test-fire the canister, don't do it into the wind because it can drift back and give you the personal experience of what a bear feels like when sprayed.

✔ Don't test-fire bear spray in bear country, where the lingering smell might actually attract bears.

✔ Each person in the party should have bear spray and keep it accessible at all times. Don't forget it when going into the woods for a nature call or leaving camp for a short fishing trip.

✔ Keep bear spray close by when cooking. It won't do you much good 100 yards away in your pack if a bear, attracted by food smells, comes into camp.

✔ Don't spray bear spray on yourself, your hiking partners, around camp, or on equipment. This might attract bears.

✔ Carry a large canister, 225 grams or more.

✔ Use a bear spray with a high level of active ingredient, 1 to 2 percent capsaicin.

✔ Make sure your bear spray is a fogger, not a stream pattern.

✔ This is not the time to go cheap. Don't go for the lowest price.

✔ Make sure you carry your bear spray in an instantly accessible place. You can buy a handy holster at most sports stores.

✔ Remember the limited range of the spray, usually 20 to 30 feet.

✔ Don't let your bear spray get extremely cold or hot. Don't leave it in a hot car all day. It could explode.

✔ Only use bear spray to deter charging or attacking bears.

✔ Airlines prohibit taking bear spray on planes and the fines are very stiff for violators, so you'll have to buy your bear spray after you've reached your destination.

✔ You might have trouble getting your bear spray across the U.S./Canada border, so once again, it might be necessary to buy more when you reach your destination. Recently, however, Canada has started allowing you to carry EPA-approved bear spray with you over the border. Most major brands of bear spray are EPA-approved.

The Bear Essentials
Using Bear Spray

Attach your bear spray to your belt or pack so it's instantly available. It won't do any good if you can't be ready to spray it in two seconds.

Draw your spray and remove the safety clip immediately upon sighting a bear at close range.

Don't attempt to spray unless the bear approaches within 30 feet.

If the bear approaches within 30 feet, give it a warning blast, placing a cloud of spray between you and the bear.

If the bear continues to approach you and gets within 20 feet, give it one or two more blasts, aiming at the face.

If the bear approaches within 10 feet, give it a five-second continuous blast, aiming directly into the bear's face and eyes. Continue to fire until the bear retreats or the canister is empty.

Special Regulations in National Parks

I strongly believe that nearly all encounters that have occurred could have been avoided, and that all future ones can be prevented.

—Gary Brown

It would be wonderful to have one checklist of things to do when venturing into bear country, but there is no chance of this ever happening. Bear populations vary their behavior, and black bears and grizzly bears often behave quite differently. As a consequence, bear-management specialists must vary regulations to match local conditions. This is especially true in national parks.

Most important, be sure to carefully check regulations, preferably getting the information you need before leaving home. This advance research allows you to acquire any special equipment you need (like a bear-resistant container) before getting to the entrance station and not being able to find what you need—or find it at a reasonable price. This preparation also saves time when you're anxious to hit the trail.

Many national parks require you to view a short video before getting a backcountry permit. This video, along with handouts, explains specific regulations for the park. In a few cases, recommendations in this book, such as information on food storage, party size, noise-making methods, or your reaction to an encounter, might not be totally in line with local regulations and recommendations. The recommendations and regulations of the local land-managing agency, such as the National Park Service, should always take precedence. For example, some parks have experienced heavy recreational use and have bear populations that have learned to retrieve food sacks hung in trees. These parks have developed more bear-resistant devices, such as metal hanging poles or large steel storage lockers installed at designated campsites. Other parks require you to carry your food in a small bear-resistant container in your backpack. Another good example is dog regulations. You can take your dog into most public lands, but most national parks prohibit dogs on back-country trails. Ditto for firearms, which are allowed on most public lands but prohibited in national parks.

Bear jams

Bear jams can be sticky situations. Don't have a false sense of security, and be careful to protect yourself and bears.

It's always a thrill to see a bear, and national parks can be a great place to view a bear safely from a roadway, but you should take special precautions. When somebody ahead of you sees a bear, they usually stop, stopping the next vehicle, and before you can blink, you're in a bear jam. If this happens to you, here are some tips on keeping yourself and the bears safe.

- If traffic is heavy, slow down or stop and be patient.
- If traffic is light, pull off the road only if there is a pullout or other safe stop. Don't stop in the middle

of the road—and watch for other drivers who might not follow this advice.

✔ Watch other vehicles and pedestrians who might be concentrating on the bear and making erratic movements such as crossing the road in front of you without checking for traffic.

✔ If you stop, don't take too much time. Traffic is backing up behind you, and you should give others a chance to see the bear.

✔ Stay in your vehicle.

✔ Never try to lure the bear closer for a photograph.

✔ Never approach the bear for a better photo or for any other reason.

✔ Never feed bears.

✔ If you see a No Stopping sign, follow this advice. Rangers may be trying to change bear behavior by avoiding bear jams. Give the bear a chance of surviving, and do not stop.

Visitors to national parks can unintentionally be responsible for the death of roadside bears. Bears that become semi-tame or stressed by people getting too close may react aggressively and cause an injury. Then, this bear might have to be killed.

Here is a partial list of parks and specific regulations that complements the general recommendations in this book.

Alaska national parks

Alaska has more bears than the rest of the United States. The state also has many national park areas, all with different regulations. It's vitally important to check park-specific regulations before traveling to Alaska to hike in any of the bear-rich parks.

Banff, Jasper, and other Canadian national parks

Bear experts from Canadian national parks reviewed the information in this book and said it fits the general bear management and advice they distribute. They recommend being particularly cautious and not having a false sense of security while viewing bears from a road.

Glacier National Park

Bear management experts in Glacier recommend using loud human voices instead of metallic noise when hiking backcountry trails.

Great Smoky Mountains National Park

Great Smoky Mountains has a healthy population of black bears, but no grizzly bears, and unlike western black bear populations, all black bears in Great Smoky Mountains are black. Bear management experts at Great Smoky Mountains do not recommend trying to burn leftovers or garbage, even if campfires are permitted. Also, since there is no chance of the bear being a grizzly, the park recommends physical resistance be used during an encounter instead of playing dead.

Grand Teton National Park

Regulations in Grand Teton National Park match most of the contents of this book, with a few minor exceptions. Many designated campsites or camping zones in Grand Teton have steel food-storage lockers or metal poles, which you should use. In some backcountry areas, you need to hang food, but officials recommend using the counter-balance method shown on page 36. Also, Grand Teton has mostly black bears (many of them brown colored) and a few grizzlies; park bear managers don't recommend trying to climb trees in case of an encounter.

Yosemite National Park

Park regulations recommend against hanging food, but it isn't illegal. Rangers are currently removing all poles and cables earlier installed for hanging food. Instead, backpackers and campers must use bear-resistant food containers. Regulations require backpackers to store food and garbage and other scented items, such as sunscreen and toothpaste, in food-storage lockers at some backcountry camps. The park also recommends storing garbage in bear-resistant containers and packing it out with you instead of trying to burn it. Food-storage canisters are mandatory when camping above 9,600 feet.

In vehicle campgrounds in Yosemite's frontcountry areas, the park requires you to store food and all other scented items in food-storage lockers provided at all campgrounds. Don't store food or scented items in vehicles, and never leave food in a vehicle overnight. If you don't need it or don't have room in the food storage locker, throw it away in a bear-resistant garbage container.

Special Precautions for Women

The risk is minimal and acceptable. We all accept some element of risk in our daily life. That risk is not appreciably higher in bear country.

—Steve Herrero

Most bear-country hiking and camping techniques apply equally to men and women; however, women should take a few extra precautions.

No smell is the best smell

As recommended earlier in this book, you should avoid strong smells when in bear country. This goes for men and women. Many feminine products, such as shampoo, however, are heavily scented. In addition to not using these strong-smelling products on the trail, refrain from using them at home the day before you plan to enter bear country. Search for unscented products, or even better, go without. You do not need cosmetics, lotion, shampoo, or perfume in the wilderness.

Menstruation

Bear experts disagree on the safety of women traveling in bear country during their menstrual periods. Some authorities recommend that women stay out of bear country during menstrual periods, but others believe this is an overreaction.

Field tests under controlled conditions have shown that bears are attracted to menstrual odor and several other strong odors. To date, however, there is no evidence that bears are attracted to menstrual odor more than they are to any other odor. In addition, no known bear attack has been traced to menstruation as a cause. Nonetheless, common sense dictates that since bears have a keen sense of smell, women should take extra precautions.

Keep yourself as clean and odor-free as possible. Use pre-moistened, unscented cleaning towelettes, and use tampons instead of pads. Never bury used tampons or towelettes. A bear could easily smell them and dig up this little "reward." This could endanger the next woman to come down the trail.

Place all used tampons and towelettes in double zip-locked bags and store them with other garbage in a bear-resistant container or hang them 10 feet off the ground.

Making the choice

There is no scientific evidence indicating that women are at greater risk during menstrual periods than they are at any other time. If you choose to go into bear country, take all special precautions as outlined above and elsewhere in this book, and enjoy the trip.

Special Precautions for Hunters, Anglers, and Outfitters

Simply put, the great bear has all the strikes against recovery that the creator could have bestowed upon it, including finding its last refuge in the well-armed West that looks to John Wayne for a role model. It is still true today that very few bears die of natural death; almost all die because we kill them.

—Louisa Willcox

This book outlines the steps you can take to make your trip to bear country as safe as possible, but if you wanted to make the trip as hazardous as possible, you would employ many techniques commonly used by hunters and anglers. Hunters want to surprise wildlife, and they work hard at being as quiet as possible. The same goes for anglers stalking a big trout in a mountain stream. Consequently, hunters and anglers must make a difficult compromise between safety and success.

For hunters and outfitters

Hunting (especially big-game hunting) can be more than hiking. Hunters silently stalk around the woods during early morning and late evening or quietly walk through bear country in darkness to reach a good vantage point before first light—in clothes laced with buck scent. Some bear experts believe bears might be attracted by gunfire, which could be associated with the presence of fresh meat or a gut pile. Even though there's a limit to what hunters can do to prevent bear encounters and still hope for any chance of hunting success, they should consider these extra precautions:

- When hiking to a favorite spot during darkness, use a flashlight.

- When camping out, select and set up the camp as described in Chapter 4.

- Don't hunt alone.

- Make extra noise when driving game out of thick brush or dense thickets of small trees.

- If you see a carcass or gut pile left by another hunter, don't go near it.

- If a big-game hunt is successful, field-dress the animal and get it out of the backcountry as quickly as possible.

- Quickly separate the carcass from the gut pile. Use a sheet of heavy plastic to move the gut pile about 100 yards from the carcass.

- Don't leave your gut pile near a trail or campsite where a bear might claim it and create circumstances that could threaten other hunters or hikers using the trail or campsite.

✔ Don't drag a carcass into camp. A bear might follow the scent trail.

✔ If you leave a carcass unattended, hang it 10 feet off the ground, which is required in some national forests. If necessary, cut the meat into smaller pieces to facilitate hanging.

✔ Hang any carcasses at least 100 yards from any campsite or trail as required in some national forests. If it's not possible to hang the carcass, cache it at least 100 yards from camp.

✔ If you can't hang the carcass, leave it on the ground in an open area where you can observe it from a safe distance when you return to claim your prize.

✔ Leave an article of clothing (ripe with human scent) on or near the carcass or pour ammonia around the carcass to deter bears.

✔ Noisily return to the carcass upwind, so the bear can get your scent before you get there. Thoroughly scan the area with binoculars before approaching the carcass. If you see that the carcass has been moved or partially buried, a bear may have claimed it. If a bear claims the carcass, abandon it and leave the area immediately.

✔ Do not attempt to shoot or harass the bear that has claimed your carcass.

✔ Use horses to decrease the chance of a bear encounter.

✔ Watch for signs of bear activity and know bear habitat.

✔ When bugling for elk, be alert. Bugling not only attracts elk, but in a few cases, bears, too.

For anglers

Anglers can also make their trip safer with a few extra precautions:

✔ Don't fish alone.

✔ Remember that bears like to travel along streams and lakeshores, so when following a loud, rushing mountain stream in thick brush, make lots of noise, preferably metallic noise like an aluminum rod case clanging on rocks.

✔ Catch-and-release fishing is much less likely to attract a bear than is having fish for dinner. Seriously consider not keeping and eating fish in bear country if you can't have a hot campfire to burn entrails and leftovers.

✔ Don't bury fish entrails. Burn them or pack them out. When fishing in large streams or deep lakes, you can clean the fish right where you catch them (instead of back at camp) and, after puncturing the air bladder, throw entrails into the deep water. Never leave entrails along lakeshores or in small streams.

✔ If you want fish for dinner, keep those you catch in the water as long as possible to keep the smell to a minimum.

✔ Don't clean fish within 200 yards of camp.

✔ Avoid getting fish odors on your clothes, and wash hands thoroughly after cleaning fish.

Special Precautions for Mountain Bikers

*Only those able to see the pageant of
evolution can be expected to value its
theater, the wilderness, or its
outstanding achievement, the grizzly.*

—Aldo Leopold

In recent years, mountain biking has become quite popular, including long excursions, sometimes with overnight stays, into bear country. In most national parks, the National Park Service only allows mountain biking on designated roads. In the national forests, the USDA Forest Service prohibits mountain biking in designated wilderness areas but allows bicycles on most other trails and roads.

Mountain bikers should, of course, carefully follow all precautions followed by backpackers, but they can take a few extra precautions to make their trip even safer.

Noise is even more important

Mountain bikers coasting down a hill can build up some major speed and, in most cases, do not make much noise, creating a hazardous situation. The speed and relative silence of biking will not alert a bear around a blind corner or small hill, setting up the circumstances for a sudden encounter. The same hazardous situation could be created while cranking up a long hill and concentrating energy on getting to the top instead of looking around or making noise.

Human voices probably won't be loud enough, so rely on metallic noise. Attach a bear bell to your saddle or handlebar. The bell will constantly clang as you ride down a bumpy trail. This will be distracting but safe. You can also buy hand-operated bells for handlebars, which you can ring whenever your visibility is impaired, such as on a long downhill with blind curves.

Moonlight bike rides are increasing in popularity, but they increase your chances of an encounter. Don't ride at night in bear country.

Special Precautions for Photographers

*We should preserve grizzly bear populations,
not because their ecological function is critical,
but because of what they can do for human
imagination, thought and experience.*

—Steve Herrero

Trying to get a good picture of a bear, especially of a grizzly, is always risky, and photographers have been mauled and killed on failed attempts to do so. Nonetheless, photographers will rarely pass up the chance to get a good bear photo. A few guidelines might make the photo attempt safer:

- Use at least a 500-mm telephoto lens.
- Avoid direct eye contact with the bear, which could be interpreted as an act of aggression.
- Don't make unusual sounds or throw anything at the bear to prompt it into a better pose.
- If the bear moves away, don't follow or chase it.
- Maintain a distance of 1,000 feet or more. But remember that under some circumstances, this can still be dangerous.

✔ Immediately retreat at any sign of the bear becoming aggressive, but don't panic and run.

✔ Be particularly cautious when photographing a female with cubs.

✔ If possible, photograph from your vehicle.

✔ In the backcountry, try to set up near a climbable tree tall enough to get you 10 feet off the ground.

✔ Never approach or try to sneak up on a bear.

✔ Never feed or leave food in an attempt to attract a bear. This is not only unethical but also dangerous for you and for other people who might come into the area at a later date.

Close Encounters

The thing that makes me very unhappy about the whole incident is my fear that this will only add fuel to the fire for those people who advocate the destruction of the grizzly to make our national parks safe. There is no reason, in the name of civilized progress, to kill an animal for doing what is natural. I feel no malice toward the bear. It was my fault for sticking my neck out too far. The bear was only protecting her young and her territory. The only thing that will prevent me from hiking in the wilderness again is the eventual destruction of the wilderness itself, and when anyone advocates the destruction of grizzlies, he is in essence advocating the destruction of the true wilderness. Let us pray that this never happens.

—Robert Hahm, 1968 mauling victim

The threat of having a close encounter with a bear is like the threat of having a heart attack. If you practice preventive health care, stay physically fit, and watch your diet, you're much less likely to have heart problems. Likewise, if you follow the safety guidelines in this book, you're much less likely to have bear problems. With both heart attacks and bear attacks, prevention is the key.

What is an encounter?

In this book, a bear sighting (seeing a bear at a safe distance) is not considered an encounter. An encounter is a situation where you may be at risk. In many cases, it's what happens when you don't follow all the recommendations listed earlier in this book. An encounter could be surprising a bear on or off the trail. It could be a bear coming into camp. It could also be an attack.

Disagreement rules the day

If you're uncertain about what to do in case of an encounter, you aren't alone. Even bear experts disagree on how to react to various kinds of encounters. Every encounter is different; every person is different; and every bear is different. Consequently, there's no checklist for what to do. Nonetheless, your reaction to an encounter can definitely affect your chances of coming away uninjured.

Defensive or offensive

The most recent recommendations from bear scientists and managers divide all encounters into two categories— defensive and offensive. Defensive encounters are situations where you suddenly come upon a bear and where a bear could be as surprised as you are. Offensive encounters are situations where a bear intentionally moves toward you. Most likely, the offensive bear is bluffing or simply curious instead of being truly aggressive or predatory.

Previously, bear managers had different recommendations for black bears than grizzly bears, but now they lump all bears together and split them up as defensive or offensive bears. In other words, you should read the behavior, not the species.

Have a rehearsal

Not many recommendations apply to all encounters, but one does—cool heads prevail. Panic is your greatest enemy. To help avoid panic, do rehearsals before you hit the trail. Go through hypothetical situations and decide what each member of the group should do. This rehearsal builds self-confidence throughout the group.

How to play dead

Bear experts used to recommend playing dead by curling up in the cannonball position, but most now recommend lying flat on your stomach with hands clasped behind your neck and elbows extended, a position that gives your vital organs as much protection as possible and makes it hard for the bear to turn you over. While playing dead, remain silent and leave your pack on—if you're already carrying one—to further protect your body. If the bear turns you over, continue rolling back onto your stomach.

Playing dead. If you're wearing a backpack, leave it on.

If you see a bear at a distance

First and most important, don't move toward the bear while you enjoy this rare and beautiful sight. If the bear is a long distance away from the trail, enjoy your wildlife viewing experience and continue down the trail. If the bear is uncomfortably close to the trail ahead but is acting naturally and not moving toward you, slowly hike back down the trail about a quarter-mile, keeping an eye on the bear until you are out of sight. Wait there fifteen or twenty minutes and then hike back up the trail making lots of noise. If the bear is still near the trail ahead and still acting naturally, take a big detour around the bear, upwind if possible, so the bear can get your scent. Stay out of sight, if possible, and make lots of noise to make sure the bear knows you're there. Then, quickly (walk, don't run) leave the area.

If you see a bear from your camp

If the bear is at a distance, get the bear spray out and make lots of noise to scare it away. If there's still time before nightfall, break camp and move to another campsite. Seeing a bear circling a camp during the day might mean that it will come into camp at night.

If the bear is close to camp, move to the base of the escape tree you previously scouted out. Take noisemakers and bear spray with you. If the bear comes closer, get up the tree. Take the food with you, if possible, so the bear doesn't get a food reward. If you don't have good escape trees or time to get up them, stand together to look bigger and more threatening to the bear and with the bear spray ready. If the bear comes dangerously close, spray it.

If you see a bear at close range

Most important, don't panic or run wildly or scream. Running or other sudden movements might cause the bear to charge. As long as you stay cool-headed and under control, you have an excellent chance of leaving this encounter with only vivid memories, not injuries. If you act like prey, you can become prey.

The first thing to do is nothing—make no sudden moves or sounds. Stand still. Be quiet. Take your bear spray from its holster and remove the safety clip. Keep your backpack on. Look around for cubs. Then, carefully assess the situation.

Watch for aggressive behavior, such as laid-back ears, hackles up on the back of its neck, head rapidly swinging from side to side, threatening "woofs," or feet slapping on the ground. If the bear mashes its teeth together making a loud "pop," it's very agitated and likely to charge. If the bear stands on its hind feet and puts its snout up, it isn't a sign of aggression. The bear is trying to get your scent or get a better look at you.

Any bear that moves toward you should be considered aggressive. This or any other aggressive behavior is your cue that the bear wants you to get out of its turf, so back away slowly, talking quietly in a monotone voice. Avoid sudden movements. Don't turn your back on the bear; instead, turn sideways to the bear if you can. Act non-threatening and submissive. Avoid direct eye contact with the bear. As you slowly retreat, slowly move your arms up and down—like doing jumping jacks without jumping. You can drop something on the trail (clothing, walking stick, etc.) to distract the bear, but not anything with food in it. You don't want to give the bear a food reward for chasing you.

If you decide to climb a tree, make sure you can reach the tree and get 15 feet up it before the bear gets there. Running toward the tree could easily prompt the bear to run after you. Remember, bears can sprint at up to 40 miles per hour. In several documented encounters, people have underestimated a bear's speed and been mauled trying to get up a tree.

If a bear charges you

It's easy to say and hard to do, but again, don't panic. Many bear charges are bluffs. Point your bear spray at the bear and stand your ground. Sometimes a bear will make several bluff charges. Don't spray the bear unless you're sure the bear isn't bluffing and is within range. If the bear stops after a bluff charge, slowly wave your arms, talk softly, and slowly back away. Again, you can drop something without food in it to distract the bear.

If the bear doesn't stop, spray it.

If the bear makes physical contact

If the bear charges and makes physical contact with you, it's important to know whether this is a defensive or offensive bear. If you surprise the bear, and it charges you suddenly out of nowhere, it's probably a defensive bear threatened by you unexpectedly appearing nearby—or it might be defending its cubs or food cache. When involved in an encounter with a defensive bear, act submissive and play dead, unless the bear becomes predatory, which is your cue to fight back with everything you can.

Let a defensive bear rough you up a bit. Don't fight back. Remain flat and silent. Don't look at the bear. If the bear moves away, be patient and continue to play dead until you're sure it has left the area. Then, quickly (no running!) move out of the area. If the bear continues to maul you while you're playing dead, you know it isn't a defensive bear after all. It's an offensive bear, so give up the game and use whatever physical resistance you can muster as a last resort.

If you know the bear has purposely moved toward you, getting closer and closer until it made physical contact with you, consider it an offensive bear. When attacked by an offensive bear, don't play dead or act submissive. Fight back with all your might and with whatever weapons you can find. It might seem futile to face an opponent many times faster and stronger than you are, but you might be surprised what you can do in a life-threatening situation. If you see one of your companions in this situation, intervene on his or her behalf.

If a bear comes into camp during daylight

A bear coming into camp is not the same type of bear that you surprise on the trail. This bear has chosen to approach you and is definitely an offensive bear. It could be a bear that has become conditioned to human food and garbage. This bear is more dangerous because it has stopped trying to avoid an encounter. The bear might not intend to attack. More likely, it's looking for another food reward. Try to prevent the bear from getting it. Allowing the bear to get more food only makes it even more dangerous for you and the next camper.

Stay calm. Avoid direct eye contact. Stay together in a close group to look bigger and more threatening than you really are to the bear. Talk softly, and slowly retreat. If you have to abandon the camp and sacrifice your camping gear, do it. Return to the trailhead and immediately report the encounter to a ranger.

If the bear moves toward you, react in the same way you would if it approached you on the trail.

If a bear comes into your camp at night

Get the bear spray ready and use your flashlight to verify that it's a bear. It might be a campground deer or one of your hiking partners looking for the bathroom.

If it's a bear and you have time to get to your escape tree, do it, but don't leave the tent if you aren't sure you have time to get up the tree. If the bear is hanging around the cooking area because of the food smell, make lots of noise and try to scare the bear away.

If a bear comes into your tent

This is the worst possible situation. It very rarely happens, but there are a few documented cases.

A night attack comes from a predatory bear. Don't act like prey. Don't lie still in your sleeping bag. Don't play dead. Don't run or scream, but don't remain calm. Instead, fight back with everything you have. Use the bear spray. Make loud noise. Shine your flashlight in the bear's eyes. Temporarily blind the bear with the flash on your camera. Whack it on the nose with your flashlight or walking stick Use whatever physical resistance you can.

Generalizations may be more dangerous than bears

The above suggestions have been boiled down from personal experience, extensive research through written literature, and many discussions with bear experts. But these are still only general guidelines. They won't work every time. Special situations and special bears won't fit guidelines.

One thing is clear: stay calm and try to rationally evaluate the situation. If you have studied up on bears and if your group has had rehearsals, you can, in most cases, safely survive an encounter.

Be realistic

After reading a few pages about how to deal with encounters, it might be harder to overcome the fear of bears, but be realistic. If you practice the methods outlined in Chapters 3 and 4, you have only the slightest chance of ever having an encounter. And even if you do, you have a good chance of coming out of it uninjured.

If bears wanted to prey on humans, it would be easy. Bears could easily kill hundreds of people, but then, of course, there wouldn't be any bears because we would've killed them all. Obviously 99+ percent of the bears only want to be separated from people. Keep this in mind as you prepare for—and then enjoy—your trip to bear country.

The Bear Essentials
Surviving an Encounter

There is no checklist on what to do; every encounter is different.

Preventing the encounter is the highest priority.

Have a dress rehearsal.

Always carry bear spray.

Cool heads prevail. Panic is your greatest enemy.

Carefully assess the situation.

Don't run from a bear.

Talk softly and slowly retreat.

Any bear coming into camp is dangerous.

A night attack comes from a predatory bear.

If you act like prey, you become prey.

Keep the risk of an encounter in perspective.

Report all encounters.

Living or Vacationing in Bear Country

Keeping bears wild keeps them alive.
Kindness kills wildness.

—Parks Canada

More and more people are moving into bear country or at least spending a week or two there on a summer vacation. Hardly a day goes by without news of a new resort or mine, most with accompanying residential developments. Second homes and wilderness cabins continue to sprout up in many privately-owned meadows in bear country. In short, more and more people are living in bear country with more and more chance of conflict with bears. If bears, and particularly grizzly bears, are to survive this forced coexistence, the residents of bear country must consider the impact their daily activities has on bears, as well as their own safety.

Your garbage could kill me

A "garbage bear" is a soon-to-be-dead bear, and somebody might get hurt along the way. If you live in or visit bear country, you must be extremely careful not to let bears get human food or garbage. You don't want to be responsible for a regrettable chain of events that could kill somebody—and probably will kill a bear.

Garbage is like bear candy, but in reality, it's bear

drugs, and in many places, still an uncontrolled substance. It might be useless waste to us, but to bears garbage has extremely high nutritional value. It only takes one garbage meal for a bear to get hooked, for bears prefer human food to natural food. The bear becomes conditioned to garbage and will go to extremes to get it. The bear will return again and again looking for more garbage. If it can't get a food reward at your place, it will go to your neighbor's place. The bear might even abandon its normal wariness of humankind and come dangerously close to people to get food or garbage. It will climb over fences, break into cabins, or rip open dumpsters and vehicles.

Sooner or later, a fed bear is a dead bear. But before the bear is killed, it might injure a child playing in a backyard or a hiker on a nearby trail. If it can't get human food from cabins, it might try getting some out of a backpacker's tent.

Everybody living in bear country bears the responsibility of keeping garbage away from bears. It goes with the territory.

Storing garbage

If you use outside garbage cans, don't put food items into them. Use outside garbage cans for nonfood items only. Better yet, keep garbage in the barn, garage, or basement, completely unavailable to bears. Try to store it in a manner that prevents odors from escaping.

Many communities and most national parks have bear-proof dumpsters, incinerators, or other approved disposal facilities. If you decide to live in bear country, take the extra time needed to haul your garbage to these facilities. You can also buy bear-resistant garbage containers for your house.

Watch the kids

Closely supervise children. They're little and helpless and might look like easy prey to bears (even more so to mountain lions). Don't allow kids to hike out of sight without adult supervision. You might be super-conscious about not creating bear–human conflicts, but do you know what your neighbors have been doing? Even if you haven't had bears visiting your place, there still could be a garbage bear in the area.

Pets and livestock

Use the same level of caution for pet and livestock food as you do for human food and garbage. Bears love horse pellets and dog food, but don't let them get it. When you feed livestock, try not to spill pellets, oats, or other food on the ground.

Honey bears

No surprise. Bears love honey. They also love the larval form of bees. If you live in bear country and have beehives, you'll probably have bear problems. Make the hives inaccessible to bears. One common method is putting the hives on platforms at least 10 feet off the ground. Use metal poles or cover the wooden support poles with tin to prevent bears from climbing up for their honey treat. You can also use electric fencing to fend off bears.

Fruits and vegetables

Fruit trees and vegetable gardens attract bears like magnets, and it's almost impossible to keep them away, especially during years when natural foods have a bad crop. If you live in bear country, you really should not plant fruit trees. In addition to creating a hazardous situation for you, your family, and your neighbors, bears that become overly bold in raiding fruit trees are usually killed.

If you have fruit trees, the best defense against bears is electric fencing. Also, try to pick all the fruit immediately after it ripens to cut down the amount of time it tempts bears. Ditto for vegetable gardens.

Compost happens

Many residents of remote areas like to use composting to cut down the amount of refuse they create. That's generally sound environmental practice, but in bear country, the odor of decomposing food in compost heaps can lure bears dangerously close to human habitations. If you live in bear country, you should not compost refuse. If you must compost, do it in an enclosed area like a garage or barn.

Bird feeders or bear feeders

Bird feeders, particularly if you use suet, can also attract bears. Only use suet in winter months when bears are having their winter sleep. Hang hummingbird feeders out of reach of bears. Take platform feeders in at night or put them on long, metal poles out of reach of bears.

The risk factors

Many people think staying close to residential communities is safer than hiking 10 miles into the wilderness. The reverse may be true.

More people always means more garbage, and if somebody hasn't used proper disposal, there could be a dangerous bear hanging around a developed area. Conversely, most hikers nowadays use zero-impact camping techniques and are very careful not to let bears get human food or garbage. A remote campsite could be safer than a backyard picnic.

The Bear Essentials

Living or Vacationing in Bear Country

Never, never, never feed bears.

Make sure bears never get human food or garbage.

Keep food odors to a minimum.

Keep bird, pet, and livestock food away from bears.

Keep compost piles in enclosed buildings.

Put electric fencing around beehives, fruit trees, and vegetable gardens.

Talk to neighbors about proper handling of garbage and other bear attractants.

Closely supervise children.

Afterword
The Parks Are Not Enough

In a deeply tribal sense, we love our monsters.
—E. O. Wilson

This book gives safety tips about protecting yourself from all bears, not only grizzly bears, but in reality, many readers tend to be most concerned about grizzly bears. This is why I choose to devote this afterword to a few personal opinions about the mightiest bear of them all, the grizzly.

Something happens to people who see a grizzly in a wild setting. It changes people. It brings a tear of joy to their eyes. It leaves a permanent impression in their psyche. I would, in fact, argue that this is the best thing you can see. Viewing a grizzly in a zoo might be enjoyable and help with identification and build some appreciation for threatened wildlife, but it's a far cry from watching a female grizzly shepherd her cubs across a mountain meadow.

I'm a lucky guy. I spend several weeks every year in grizzly country, and I've seen lots of wild grizzly bears. I also spend countless hours reliving those magnificent moments.

I have taken my children into the heart of the wilderness with the specific goal of seeing a grizzly. They saw several, and they'll always carry those life experiences with them. Now, my children are all grown up and going out to see grizzlies on their own. They're also having their own babies and will soon be taking them out to see a wild grizzly.

In thirty-five years of hiking, mostly in grizzly country, I have had one serious encounter and a few sightings that were close enough to get the adrenaline flowing. Every detail of these experiences is permanently etched in my memory and helped prompt me to write this book.

But there is a problem with all of this. As more and more hikers, hunters, anglers, mountain bikers, and climbers do what I do and continue to penetrate the last remnants of the grizzly's domain, they place more and more stress on this threatened symbol of the wilderness. Every day it becomes harder and harder for the big bear to avoid us. Actually, this is also true for the black bear throughout its range, including more populated eastern states and around eastern national parks, such as Great Smoky Mountains.

We can all be part of the solution, instead of part of this problem. I have confidence that most people interested in going deep into the mountains want to help preserve the king of those mountains, the majestic grizzly bear. That's why we have an obligation to know how to avoid and react to an encounter because that unfortunate meeting might result in the death of a bear. We should not only be concerned with our own welfare. Our carelessness can create a "problem bear," which is, of course, a sympathetic name for a soon-to-be-dead bear.

Even worse, perhaps, is the fact that each headline about a bear mauling makes us more afraid of grizzlies and perhaps less certain we want them around. That's why it is so vital for all of us to be bear aware. By doing so, we not only protect ourselves and individual bears, but also help preserve a future for the species.

I also have confidence that anybody who gets a glimpse of a wild grizzly will be a strong supporter of wilderness from that moment on. In some cases it might be enough to simply go to where the grizzly walks and sense the presence of the most majestic of animals. Trust me, you can feel it.

The grizzly needs your help. The grizzly needs lots of room, and civilization is gradually erasing the last blank spots on the map. The national parks are large, but not large enough. The grizzly needs more than the parks. We need to accept the bear in large tracts of western landscape not designated as national parks.

So, in conclusion, the grizzly needs two things from us. The great bear needs all the wild, roadless habitat we have left, and the grizzly needs to be accepted and revered instead of feared or hated. The grizzly needs you.

Appendix

Much of the information in this appendix came from Patti Sowka at the Living with Wildlife Foundation, which contracts with bear managers to keep a current list of manufacturers and sources of bear-resistant products and to coordinate testing and certification protocol. You can find the resource guides on www.lwwf. org or on CD-ROM. Contact the foundation at the following address:

Living with Wildlife Foundation
P.O. Box 1152, Swan Valley, MT 59826
(406) 754–0010; psowka@blackfoot.net

Sources of Bear Spray
These companies sell EPA-registered bear deterrent sprays. Manufacturers not registered by the EPA have not been included.

Bear Guard
Guardian Personal Security Products, Inc.
21639 North 14th Avenue, Phoenix, AZ 85027
(800) 527–4434; guardianproducts@worldnet.att.net;
    www.guardianproducts.com

Counter Assault
Bushwacker Backpack & Supply Co., Inc.
120 Industrial Court, Kalispell, MT 59901
(800) 695–3394; original@counterassault.com;
    www.counterassault.com

Frontiersman Bear Attack Deterrent
Security Equipment Corp.
330 Sun Valley Circle, Fenton, MO 63036
(314) 343–2000; sabre@stlnet.com; www.sabredefensesprays
    .com

Guard Alaska
McNeil River Enterprises, Inc.
750 West Diamond, Suite 203, Anchorage, AK 99515
(888) 419–9695; randy@guardalaska.com; www.guardalaska
.com

UDAP Pepper Power
Universal Defense Alternative Products
13160 Yonder Road, Bozeman, MT 59715
(800) 232–7941; bearman@udap.com; www.udap.com

Sources of Bear-Resistant Food Containers

The Interagency Grizzly Bear Committee has certified the products of these companies.

Backpacker's Cache
Garcia Machine (backpacking)
14097 Avenue 272, Visalia, CA 93292
(209) 732–3785; www.backpackercache.com

The Bear Keg
Counter Assault
Bushwacker Backpack & Supply Co., Inc.
120 Industrial Court, Kalispell, MT 59901
(800) 695–3394; original@counterassault.com; www.counter
assault.com

Tahoe
Purple Mountain Engineering (backpacking)
41236 Elsdale Place, Palmdale, CA 93551
(601) 722–4936; www.purplemountainengineer.com

Bearikade Weekender
Wild Ideas (backpacking)
P.O. Box 1575, Santa Ynez, CA 93460
(805) 693–0550; www.wild-ideas.net

LMI Welding (horse-packing)
P.O. Box 772, Cut Bank, MT 59427
(800) 345–5623; www.lmiwelding.com

Wyoming Outdoor Industries (backpacking and horse-packing)
1231 13th Street, Cody, WY 82414
(800) 725–6853; www.wyomingoutdoor.com

Wind River Products (backpacking and horse-packing)
#4 Absaroka Court, Dubois, WY 82513
(307) 455–2464

Sources of Bear-Resistant Garbage Containers

McClintock Metal Fabricators
455 Harter Avenue, Woodland, CA 95776
(800) 350–3588; sales@mcclintockmetal.com; www
  .mcclinkockmetal.com

Haul-All Equipment Systems
4115 18th Avenue North, Lethbridge, Alberta, Canada
  T1H 5G1
(800) 661–1162; sales@haulall.com; www.hualall.com

UnBearable Bins
P.O. Box 1313, Bragg Creek, Alberta, Canada T0K 0K0
(403) 609–2242; ubbins@telus.net; www.unbearablebins.com

Portable Electric Fences

Gallagher Electric Fencing Products
130 W. 23rd Ave., P.O. Box 7506, North Kansas City,
  MO 84116
(800) 531–5908; info@gallagherusa. com;
  www.gallagherusa.com

Margo Supplies
P.O. Box 5440 High River, Alberta, Canada T1V 1M5
(403) 652–1932; info@margosupplies.com; www.margo
supplies.com

Specialized Products for Hanging Food
Williams Products
2825 Rehberg Lane, Billings, MT 59102
(800) 522–8930

NATPRO
P.O. Box 1076, Lander, WY 82529
(307) 332–3068

Bear Conservation Organizations
Great Bear Foundation
802 East Front Street, P.O. Box 9383, Missoula, MT
59802
(406) 829–9378; gbf@greatbear.org; www.greatbear.org

Be Bear Aware
P.O. Box 8289, Missoula, MT 59807
(406) 721–8985; bearinfo@qwest.net; www.bebearaware.org

Natural Resources Defense Council
P.O. Box 70, Livingston, MT 59047
(406) 222–9561; llwillcox@nrdc.org; www.nrdc.org

Sierra Club Grizzly Bear Ecosystems Project
P.O. Box 1290, Bozeman, MT 59771
(406) 582–8365; grizzly.bear@ sierraclub.org; www.sierra
club.org/grizzly

Defenders of Wildlife
1130 17th Street, NW, Washington, DC 20030
(800) 385–9712; info@defenders.org; www.defenders.org

Living with Wildlife Foundation
P.O. Box 1152, Swan Valley, MT 59826
(406) 754–0010; psowka@blackfoot.net

Suggested Reading
Bear Attacks: Their Causes and Avoidance
by Stephen Herrero
The Lyons Press

Where the Grizzly Walks
by Bill Schneider
Falcon Publishing

Leave No Trace
by Will Harmon
Falcon Publishing

Videos
Staying Safe in Bear Country and *Working in Bear Country,*
available from Magic Lantern Communications, (800) 263–
1717 or east@maagiclantern.ca in the United States or eastern Canada; (800) 263–1818 or west@magiclantern.ca
from western Canada; 800-667-1500 or info@mlcworld
.com from outside Canada and United States.
www.magiclantern.com.

Bear Attack: The Predatory Black Bear and *Bear Attack:
Encountering Grizzlies* available from Ellis Vision at (416)
924–2186 or sales@ellisent.com.

On the Internet
www.lwwf.org
Living With Wildlife Foundation

www.fs.fed.us/r1/wildlife/igbc
Interagency Grizzly Bear Committee

About the Author

Bill Schneider has spent thirty-five years hiking trails all across America. During college in the mid-1960s, he worked on a trail crew in Glacier National Park and became a bear addict. He spent the 1970s publishing *Montana Outdoors* magazine for the Montana Department of Fish, Wildlife and Parks—and getting out into bear country as much as possible. Bill has written eighteen books and more than one hundred magazine articles on wildlife, outdoor recreation, and environmental issues, and he has taught classes on bicycling, backpacking, zero-impact camping, and hiking in bear country for the Yellowstone Institute, a nonprofit educational organization in Yellowstone National Park. In 2000, Bill retired as president of Falcon Publishing, now part of The Globe Pequot Press, which has grown into the premier publisher of outdoor recreation guidebooks with more than 800 titles in print. Bill lives in Helena, Montana, with his wife, Marnie, and works as a publishing consultant and freelance writer.